WEEKLY READER BOOKS presents

What Is a Wave?

A **Just Ask** Book

by Chris Arvetis
and Carole Palmer

illustrated by
Vernon McKissack

FIELD PUBLICATIONS
MIDDLETOWN, CT.

Water in the ocean moves up and down.
Look at the birds bobbing up and down in the water.

Let's study a wave.
The highest point is
called the **crest**.
The lowest part between
the waves is called
the **trough**.

As the wave gets closer to shore, the ocean is not as deep.

The bottom part of the wave drags along the bottom of the ocean.

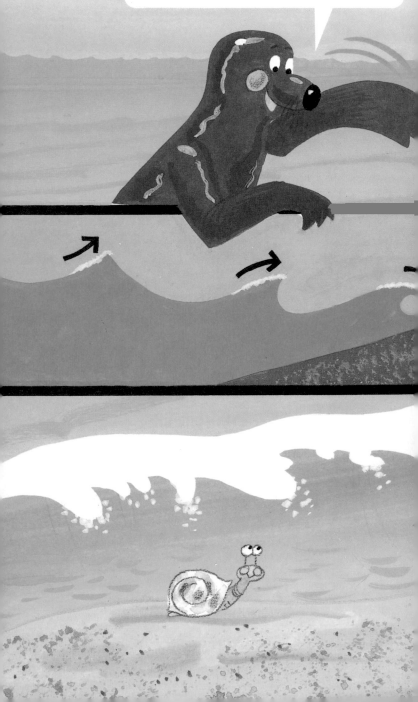

The water rushes up on the shore, pushes the sand, and splashes on the rocks.
Then the water from the wave rushes back into the ocean.

You asked what causes waves.
Well, most waves are
caused by wind.

The kind of waves the wind
makes depends on
—how strong the wind is,
—how long the wind blows,
—how much ocean the wind
  blows over.

When such a giant wave is out in the ocean, it causes few problems.

But as the wave gets to shore, it can cause lots of water to wash onto the land.

The water may cause floods and damage to houses and towns along the coast.

Waves are also caused
by gravity.
Gravity is the force that
holds things on earth
in place.
Gravity causes ocean tides
which make the water go
higher and lower.